Dream Keeper

Whyte Ivee Bel

BookLeaf
Publishing

India | USA | UK

Made with ❤ on the BookLeaf Publishing Platform
www.bookleafpub.in
www.bookleafpub.com

Dedication

Every so often,
A stranger walks in your life,
And pulls you up.
To friendships & partnerships,
To the ones who stand by us.

Preface

I have always loved the idea of a seed sprouting. Despite the darkness, it pushes its root deeper and shoots towards the light, growing within while reaching for the sky.

This is how Dream Keeper sprouted. Some of these poems formed over the years, others were carried through whispers in the air. Some were born out of pure imagination, yet others through bare emotions.

We are just as alike as we are unique and what binds us is our humanity. Dream Keeper is a journey towards that realisation.

Writing these poems have brought a range of emotions and sharing them brought a whole another set — foreign, yet familiar.

If you are reading this, know that it was once but a dream. If any of these poems strike a chord in you, the book is then a success for me.

Acknowledgements

My gratitude to the muses who occasionally showered me with inspiration, the readers who will hopefully understand and give me reasons to write more acknowledgements, and the notes app on my phone for not running out of patience with me.

Dreams

Shaping out the constellations,
As if our fingers were magic wands,
Bringing imagination to life,
What the bright sky cannot.

Bathing in the bliss of the moon and the stars,
Melodic notes hanging in the air,
Stillness falls and somnolence takes over,
As we dream of the world afar.

Here again, under the stars,
I still dream of that world afar.

Paper boats

We wished it rained more,
So we could sail our paper boats,
In the puddles everyone fussed about,
We'd jump and cheer aloud.

Soaked to bones and running around,
We'd paint the town red like clowns.
Days lived with a light heart,
What was it if not a prismatic art?

Every day is a different shade,
But I wish for more rainy days,
To sail those paper boats,
And watch the puddles fill in the road.

Memories

I stood in the middle of a meadow,
And heard a faint echo,
It came from a distant source,
I was running towards it with a mighty force.

From somewhere known it came,
I saw a blinding light, aflame,
An inexplicable reverie,
It was a beautiful memory.

He held me in warm embrace,
I looked up to see his face,
And heard him whisper my name,
Something sacrosanct it became.

An inexplicable reverie,
It was a beautiful memory.

My coloniser's tongue

My coloniser's tongue, oh still a mystery,
What a roller coaster, much like our history.

A tale of the traveler across borders and time,
Here, borrow a word, there a line.

Spread over far and wide,
Each time, watch the worlds collide.

A tussle to conquer and reign supreme,
Divide, rule and destroy every dream.

Much has changed with the passage of time,
Forgotten and forgiven almost every crime.

Valiant were those who laid their lives,
'Tis for them, my motherland thrives.

Much was witnessed by this holy ground,
But what goes around must come around.

A quarter of a century since my colonizers returned,
But their tongue, I still learned.

Oblivious to the stories of my lineage, my tribe,
A quality inherited — the good you must imbibe.

Beauty, I find in all languages,
As I encounter them at various stages.

My country so vast and diverse,
A new dialect, a vibrant canvas.

Today, I met a sister of another tongue
A sweet song with her words she strung.

As her language I began to pursue,
Our colonisers' tongue she too knew.

Hearts & Minds

Even if our minds forget, do our hearts ever?
No, we don't, says the heart,
But we must, says the mind.
It is the only way to live and prosper,
If not, how else will we ever get stronger?

Love is what we need, says the heart,
No, survival is all there is, says the mind.
It is the only way to go through life,
If not, how else will we ever thrive?
Feelings are all we need, says the heart,
Thinking is all there is, says the mind.

In different directions they flow,
Different parts of the being they care for.

So think all you must, help us keep afloat, dear mind,
Do all you must, take us to new heights.
For all that there is to cherish,
I shall remember, says the heart.
So even if our minds forget, never will our hearts, ever.

Stories untold

I have come this far and farther more to go,
Halt; Halt I must, to see what became of the seeds I
sowed.
Elusive are the ways and how, I know not.
"Come along, let us show you", said the reapers of my
gold.

Dubious and inquisitive, I let them lead,
Presumed devastated trails let it not be.
Labeled a storm, all they are capable of is a wasteland,
Arriving at an arcadia, in the moonlight I stand.

Pleasant aroma floated in the air,
The flowers in the wild had fared.
Sweet was the peace,
Sweeter still, the fruit of those industrious weeks.

Recounting the days of old,
We rejoiced in the stories untold.
Dancing and celebrating the night away,
Not all was forgotten and gone.
Recounting the days of old,
Happy was all.

The night

Like a dragon breathing fire,
The lightning threatened to strike.
Withholding a thunderous desire,
Raging among the clouds is a strife.

O, what shall become of this night?
My gaze still affixed to the sky,
How long till the daybreak brings in light?
Is it rage or joy or battle cry?

Witnessed often the blue and white,
Racing through like blood in the veins of life,
The stripes of red roar with a different might,
Amidst the angry clouds, o, how the night thrives.

Fragrance of the living

Do not bring me flowers
Do not steal their lives for me
Instead, take me to the gardens
With your favorite flowers
With my favorite flowers
Sit beside me on a bench
Let the floral scent surround us
Let's watch them in their blooming glory
And admire them as they are —
Connected to their roots
Smiling at the sky
Alive.

Free spirits

An ode to the spirits on the other side,
To where I've never dared take a ride,
Though there was a quiet confidence in my stride,
Guiding me through every low and high tide,
But crossing the shore, never did I decide,
Because the grass was always greener on my side.

But today, spirit wild and free,
Today I see,
The fire that burns in you,
The courage world prefers you to hide,
You shout and let it out.
Come world, come and see,
I'm a spirit, wild and free.

Today, I tip my hat to you spirit,
Cause you've finally made me see,
Never was it easy,
but while quiet, calm courage was always with me,
Your spirit, wild and free,
Remains a distant reverie.

Possessions

I've kept them all.
The words, the emotions,
The written, the spoken,
To revisit on the days
When everything's open —
The past, the future,
The now and myself.
I've kept them all.

La vie en rose

Wherever I look, I see those amber eyes,
That charming smile, even in the darkest of nights,
Thoughts, growing like dandelions,
My feet dancing in a sweet delirium.

Wherever I look, I see those amber eyes,
Out of the mist, under the purple skies,
Ma vie, Ma vie en rose,
It's all colours and rainbows.

Wherever I look, I see those amber eyes,
Deep from the memories they always rise,
Spreading blue feathers, ready for a flight,
A blue jay, emerging from the night.

The third charm

If we shall ever meet again,
Let this time be the charm,
Be in the right place, at the right time,
Leaving our missed chances behind.
Say, what have the years brought,
Save for the time when we were not
Meant to be and drifted apart,
But I've nailed my colours to the mast,
If I shall ever meet you again,
I won't pass you by a third time,
Because I've been told to mark,
The third time's a charm.

What makes a gentlewoman?

No lady of senior rank or birth but
She held doors for everyone else.
Made space for those in need
Because it fed a part of her being.

No lady in casual coats or expensive suits but
She shared her humble fortune.
Feeding the starved on the streets
Because it fed a part of her being.

No grande dame, never a leading lady
She supported from shadows but never greedy.
Kind disposition with clever intuition,
Some say, she was a gentlewoman.

Milestones

Chasing the days gone by, it is now that I realise,
Greener was the spring, and summer alive.
Carefree and whole, kicking leaf litter on that stroll,
Something unforgettable about that fall
And winter was unbearably cold.

Chasing the days gone by, it is now that I realise,
Radiant and animated that all was, grey and withered it
now is.
Silence that was once serene, I have heard its screams.
Something unforgettable about that stroll
And soon it'll be time to go.

Chasing the days gone by but now I realise,
Time can't rewind. Changed are you and me when I look
behind.
Perhaps when we are old, and I, no longer spent and
lost,
Remind me, what was unforgettable about
All the milestones we crossed.

Let it rain

The sun shone bright, the wind blew by,
It was one of those days, my favorite kind.
Bright but not too warm, windy but not chilly.

By the time I realised, half the day has passed by,
Now with a grey cloud hovering above my head,
Lost, doomed and helpless.

How did I end up here?
Questioning every choice at every stage,
Perhaps they are why I find myself in this dreary maze.

I try and console myself,
Those were choices in the past,
If so regretted, there is another way.

How complicated though, are our thoughts,
Feeding on the hopes fueled by those memories,
Wishing to make possible the unwritten.

After many a pensive nights and cloudy days,
Finally now I see that today is a sunny day.
Let me, let this dull cloud burst and let it rain.

Let me, let this dull cloud burst and let it rain.
Because only then, can I enjoy my favorite weather
today
And if the clouds do reappear, it'll be a tale for another
day.

Mistakes

Consumed by a dream that
Was never mine to begin with,
Not strong enough to resist it at first,
Not strong enough to fight
For it when it mattered.
Maybe it was a mistake.
But it was mine to make.

Steady

Panicking. Anxious. Muddled.
It's never going to be a smooth path,
That doesn't mean that it's not the right one.
Look ahead, move forward.

Now that I've done enough,
Tried, failed and fallen,
With these endless thoughts,
What ifs and nots.

It's as if silence knows me way too well,
It sings a lullaby to brush away my fears.
This is my perfect escape, a safe space,
Something peaceful, something grey.

Commuovere

So I will take you for a book I read,
With excitement, anticipation, longing and comfort.
Your sad eyes are happy again,
I was only a bridge
To lead you to what you became.
Now I place you safely on my shelf,
With all the others that I have read,
To either be forgotten or reread,
But forever on my shelf.

Lost but found

Treading at the edge of madness,
Swaying between the radiance and darkness,
To be lost forever and never found,
Whirling like a dervish, spellbound.
Oblivious infinity or enchanting fantasy,
Somewhere beyond you and me,
Falling under the force of gravity
Is my sanity —
Boundless,
Free,
Lost,
But found.

A lover of life

A lover of life tangled in a fierce tango
With the ultimate demise and I watch
The burning passion romancing
The impassive night and I watch
The light diminish from the gaze of
The lover of life and the music stops.

Murmur of surprise around the room
A groomed knight – role of the giver of life
He assumed and I watch
The cold revive from the warmth, waltzing
A new rhythm forming, new possibility unfolding and I
watch
Them getting acquainted and inquiring
About the former partner and the laughter stops.

We've met a few times, said the lover of life, each time
Brutal reminders of this ephemeral life
And none alone
We shall all cross the same shore
Of all the hands we held and watched turn cold
Of all the flames that burned and blown out
Of all the love given and grieved
I've been dancing all along, bereaved

My heart, at times it fade, but a spark
Can set it ablaze, and I smile
Tangled however I with the great demise
I remain
A lover
A Lover of Life.

Letters

Post the letters tanned yellow with age,
Sitting in the dust, waiting in a package,
'Cause I am old fashioned, and love,
Nothing is sweeter than receiving a letter from the
beloved.

Grief

You were in the wind that steadied me on the swing,
A familiar melody, the lullaby that no one else could
sing,
Enchanted, with my eyes closed, I swung,
I felt your presence while your absence burned.

We meet in my dreams, the ones I wish never to wake up
from,
Like a shadow – unfazed, unfaded and alive you come.

The light blinds, the noise surrounds and the spell break,
The wind still, the melody gone and the swing stops,
Now that I have grieved you for so long,
Is it alright if I finally let life move on?

The waiting

Stationed like a soldier at the door,
Waiting for her man to return home.
To bring parts of the world he had seen,
For her to paint in vibrant colors in dreams.
Stationed like a woman at the door,
Watching the troop carrier take her man far off.

Stationed like a mother at the door,
Waiting for her sons to return home.
To hold them close and to care,
To make up for the seasons they didn't share.
Stationed like a valiant at the door,
Watching them follow in the footsteps their father once
followed.

Stationed like a grandmother at the door,
Watching her grandchildren come home.
To shower them forever with her love,
Drawing the line so the world couldn't deny her.
Stationed like a guardian angel at their door,
She watched them grow old.

History

As I grow older, I often wonder about you,
The lost knowledge, your point of view,
The chances we never got, a future unlived,
But what's more, a person with a past went unnoticed.

Who were you? How were you?
A million other questions, all about you,
More important, am I anything like you?
Alas, gone before I could pose these questions to you.

As I grow older, I look for the clues,
In the mirror, the work, the art, the life,
Always putting together two and two,
Trying to live while carrying this ever growing residual
love for you.

Perhaps when this is all over,
We will be granted a chance to see each other.
Then I shall tell you, how much I have loved you.
Then I shall ask you, everything about you.

Maybe it's not hope at all

The wait and the hope,
The anxiety and the wild helpless thoughts,
The torn-apart heart smiling at the bittersweet
memories,
The missing beat at the mention of your name.

Mind screaming with countless thoughts,
The outward apparent calmness but a deceiving facade.
How trivial, the words for transient times
Elusive thoughts of the past for a future never meant to
be mine.

And yet I find myself in the state of constant paradox,
Trying to hold on when everything's telling me to let go.
Convincing myself to accept the only solution I think of,
Hold on to the memories but let go of the pain.

Oh, how easily I tell myself this,
As if I momentarily forget,
Do the memories even remain the same,
If I let go of the pain?

Grow around it, make it a part of my being,
Maybe as a mark of honour to your memories.

But these fragments, how I ever bare,
To anyone else after what we shared?

Though crushed, indestructible, the hope lives on,
Poisoning my heart, maybe not hope at all.
Intense, stubborn, persistent, still clinging on,
Attached, do I dare defy or deny?

Now a part of me, grow around,
Live on. It is all I can do.
For me. For the memories and hope,
Or something that is not hope at all.

Chapters end

A fresh chapter, a different character,
Couple of chapters in, already closer to ending,
Leading to a brand new beginning, twisting and turning,
Another chapter, another character.

Some end with grace, others precipitate,
Insatiable, satiable, wistful, mirthful,
Flawless, flawed, attract, estrange,
But they end, so another could begin.

You, one of them, a happenstance,
Albeit fleeting, was a jolly greeting,
With gratitude I have walked you till the end of this
story,
For this is the final chapter, and I am the last of
characters.

The town

The town is still brimming with the days of our youth,
When our paths converged in time,
An unspoken promise, the moment's vice.
The moment, frozen in time like a painting in my mind,
Each stroke that I now analyse.

Then we met again as if it was fate,
Something brewing under the surface,
The locked gazes, the secret language,
And the beating of my heart,
But then, it all passed.

The time, the town and the days of our youth,
Reduced to a mere recollection of what used to be,
Every street, every turn, every road,
I walk through them once more,
Traversing a sea of faces but none yours,
And just like that, this town was mine no more.

The core

I have lost the fire
That burned in the core of my heart,
Hotter than the bluest of flames,
The raging, vigorous and once eternal.

I sit vigilant over the serenity of peace,
Surrounded by the dried and dying leaves,
Waiting to catch the crackling of a spark,
To be set alight and rise from this discordant dark.

An Orison

Brief as it was, two worlds collide,
Shards of each seep into each other.

Is this now our time, our fate?
Or will this too abate?

All that can be, should be, would be,
Now is all that could have been.

When it all clears and the traces disappear,
Look through and the orisons will appear.

A part of you that you so generously shared,
Shall always be held close and treasured.

Home

Where is your home?
To whom do you belong?
Many asked me yesterday,
Years have passed since I lost my way.

In those streets I used to roam,
With my brothers and sisters I used to play.
The innocence of childhood known to us all,
Where do you think in adult it goes?

I saw the big buildings,
The smooth asphalt roads,
No more bumps on Tonga
On that dirt road.

Take me home for I will show you the way,
Somewhere I have not been, but always wish to stay,
To a place that live in my memories,
Colorful, soulful and alive.

The city

I once roamed this city —
Asleep. Ignorant of its vices.
The air refused to kiss the nature
The trees stopped dancing to its direction.
I circled the city in a gloomy stillness
Every door closed, every heart shut.
At the end of its hush, sat a man
In his old chair, with impaired vision.
Hearing my footsteps, he smiled,
And in a blink, the city woke up.

Hope

A tiny sliver, no matter how bleak,
Make us hold on so tight;
Giving us a 'why' to figure out a 'how'
To build up the strength to add meaning to life.
All our aspirations, dreams and actions,
All vague without it, for our world rests on it.
No matter how hard we try to let it go
We find ourselves still clinging on.
The smallest of the smallest dose
Suffices for the heftiest
Though it may not be practical
We crave for it to linger.
So tell me then...
Hope...
Is it dangerous too
or merely powerful?

Spark

A spark in the dark, a fire in your heart.
Fidgety night, zealous light,
Square one, either hope or run,
'Cause in life, it's never black or white.

A spark in the dark, let that fire start,
Embark on a journey, while still sunny,
Hop to the next square, might find something there,
'Cause in life, all you can do is dare.

A spark in the dark, let the fire restart,
Burn down the guards, ones around your heart,
Keep moving on, reach where you belong,
'Cause in life, there is never enough time.

A fire in your heart, let it leave a mark,
Peaceful night, zealous light,
End line, what a beautiful climb,
'Cause in life, it's all about how you arrive.

Rhythm

Play the keys, I want to hear the melody,
Light up the fire, let me feel that ecstasy,
Match my rhythm, let's dance like we're one,
Until we're lost and there is none.

Salvation

The truth does not demand more than to be told
Liberated from beneath the countless layers
From the colourful wisp of smoke of lies
To be felt in our hearts and lighten the burden
And save us from ourselves.

The war hero's wife

O, the war hero's wife, what wars have you won?
While he was on the warfront, what wars went unsung?
Once dreamy and young, what of you did become?
Fighting was he for the nation, but life of yours came
undone.

O, dear wanderer, why have you come? asked she,
Asking me of the days from which I wish to be free.
O, the war hero's wife, I came as no one's choice,
I do not spill, or fill any pocket with coins.

It was scarcity we fought, of bravery, laughter and
defence,
Whilst our children slept, we defended homes of our
men.
For those who would never return to their family,
We mourned. We prayed. We got our hands dirty.

O, dear wanderer, it was not I alone,
It became the story of every household.
We burned the bloody pyres of our blessedness alone,
The shroud on our living bodies was for us to atone?

No, there was no pity we were shown,

You can't judge us for we were not in the wrong,
We had to shed our motherly roles
So no one could break our children's souls.

O, the war hero's wife, my mother survived the same
war,
She talked of a woman whose blood was gold,
A phenomenon that happens once in a while,
You are the source of her child's smile.

I am a flower from you garden,
Because of you, peaceful was the world in which we
grew.
With respect I came for you to know,
In the tales my mother recounted at nights,
A hero who always come to their rescue.
This hero was no man, no,
She was a woman who saved so many more.
I came for you to know,
You were the war hero.
I came for you to know,
You are, my hero.

The minority

Look around you, do you see the odd one out?
The one who is oblivious to the ways of the world,
Engaged in an inner dialogue,
Fighting off the wars they would never serve.
Their vigour noticeable to those who observe.
They are enviable to most and admirable to few,
Do you see them, the ones who wished no one knew?

Look around you, do you see the stranger in your kith
and kin?
The one who is the talk of the town, but never fits in,
The hermit, the loner, the introverted,
Constantly reminded of what the real world is,
So they participate in it from a distance,
Do you see them, the ones with no offense or pretenses?

Look around you, do you see?
We are not the ones who wish to be found,
We are not the ones who wish to be a part of the crowd.

Look around you, who do you see?
Is it everyone else or the minority?

Fear

You asked me if I ever tried?
Know that I did.
I wore your shoes
And walked countless miles each night
And yet, it was never enough.
The bruises sustained in hope of healing yours
My biggest fear of not becoming like you came true
And yet, it was never enough.
So if I turn away from you, and choose myself
Would you ever try the size that doesn't fit you?

Dilemma

An unusual story it was for her
Maybe not the only of the like
Of course each unfolding is unique
And if it were to be done again,
It would have its modifications.

Each story starts way before we know
Because interconnections seem prevalent so.
We decide the length to tell,
The beginnings, end and bends as well.

Let's begin with young and naive
Although if you reflect,
No story is possible without a bit of recklessness
Strong willed though lacking exposure
Was a great decision, according to her.

So blossomed a connection among them
Good starts are imperative most times
Whether it was, depends on your wise
High and low, low and high
It more often than not was a compromise.

An expiration date soon would arrive

Before that many an events would follow course
Perhaps it was the naivety or just optimism
Compassion came but never empathised.

Between these waves a lot more interspersed
Experiences unknown and new, a new world opened
The old was questioned, dissected and disintegrated
As it seemed to have lesser and lesser merit.

This would probably be a point of heartbreak,
But this was no usual case.
Perhaps, out of the two, one did break but
For her, there was nothing left to bare.

Through the now open window she sore
New heights that she was proud of.
A sense of serenity though, all do crave
In this new scene, she relied on him.

A wonderful place it was for them
Absorbing the wonder of each day
The rainbow slowly revealed through
The starts and glowing treetops that
Seemed to exist only for them.

'Time' was an abstract as could be
A short span had more wonder than a long compromise

A tough decision through loomed awhile
It had to be made for it was right.

The flow carried on though the variation of waves
intensified
Trying to catch up, she hoped the waves would be kind.
Hoped and hoped but reminded of her decision,
She knew she was right but still hoped for a different
direction.

The end was near but was it already here?
Uncertainty is uncomfortable but she wasn't brave
enough
To ask the questions she didn't want answers to
Though she empathised, she felt the shatter
But also wise enough to know with that time she would
revive.

It feels like only yesterday

It feels like only yesterday,
When I saw the reflection in your eyes,
The shades of green
against the bright yellow and white,
Pausing to etch the memory of the studded shore
as the traffic rushed us by.

It feels like only yesterday,
That I smelled the future nostalgia,
The unexpected scent that
I had no idea I'd grow to cherish
And I collected the smell to keep
which now only lingers in my memory.

It feels like only yesterday,
The sensation of cold food on a cold day,
The exotic experiments as the crowds blur away,
The absence of hunger
And the passage of time.

It feels like only yesterday,
Your firm, gentle touch
Reassured me despite the spats.
Arms around a little too tight but

That's what felt exactly right.

It feels like only yesterday,
The soothing sound of your jumbled words,
Turned a hurt soul's symphony.
The solace in the familiar voice sharing stories
of times both drab and of glory.

And it feels like only yesterday,
That brave and stupid lived,
But cherished and alive they remained.
And it feels like only yesterday,
That it was yesterday,
That you really were here.

Kindly cruel or cruelly kind?

How cruel could you be?
Force something on me
That I never wanted
Fought and resisted but
Then finally accepted.
CRASH.

No my dear, your fight isn't over,
Not so soon, not ever.
For as long as you live, I'll be here,
Making sure you always strive.

I thought we were friends, my dear life!
How I cling to you, struggle to survive
Go the extra mile, hold on just to stay alive
Knowing fully well that we too are on limited time.

Yes my dear, fight for me
I'm my greatest irony!
I am the game and the very reward,
Simple as can be but never easy.

Take me high, drown me low,
I will thrive wherever we go.
In sync, how wonderfully we flow
Couldn't we find a balance so?

Hahaha! No!
Careful dear! Steady! Down you go
The way back up, you might think you know,
But it will be harder, each time you grow.

You can't be serious?
Is this your idea of a joke?
Yanking and crashing, to and fro,
How far could I possible go?

Oh I don't know either,
Let's find out together.
Give it just one more try,
You might just come out alive.

I will, dear life. Steady myself and rise,
Cruel as you are, I know you'll be kind
So I'll always fight, to meet you up there,
Your irony beyond my grasp, yet I'll climb.

Welcome back, you've reached your peak,
Ready to set sight on the next you seek?

How long will you stay this time?
Will it finally be your turn to shine?

Dear life, why are you so kind to bring me up,
When just as cruelly, you'll make me give up?
Never mind, tough competition though you might be,
I'm ready to play, let's bring out the best in me.

Death knell

I want to write something profound,
Hold captive that is not yet a sound,
These thoughts are like hounds,
Chasing something wild, refusing to turn around.

Who is their prey? No, it would not show,
What haunts the living, to whom do they bow?
When the last knell is heard and the clock strike an
obituary,
What is it that move when all else is stationary?

Tilted on a vulnerable axis rest all the weight,
In-between space, from this to that resting place,
At last, every breath, a hope before peace prevailed,
The axis tilt yet again, cried in the dusk a lonely
nightingale.

I want to convey, I want to form a sound,
I want to say something profound,
But how my words fail me now,
Oh, how my words fail me now.

Memorial

53

The memories speak,
A shadow looming in the distance,
An echo in the dark,
Eyes shut and the vision clears.

Time runs out,
Moments fade away,
Deep slumber calling,
To the final destination.

Born from this world,
Gone from it one day,
From flesh to ashes will this life lead,
All I wish for you is to love every day.

Unknown artist

Behind every coat of paint on this wall
is an unknown artist.
Behind every brush stroke on this easel
is an intention, tarnished.

Peel of the layers, one at a time,
reveal if it was shame or the ruins.
Reveal, from different walks of life,
the intention behind every drawing.

Lo and behold, the layers falling off,
The unknown artist's time rewind.
Decades later, then decades before,
if only it was an illusion and nothing more.

Face to face with different ages,
from tranquility to an undertone of rage,
then doodles, a sign of courage?
Perhaps, it was neither ruins nor shame.

It was neither ruins nor shame.
It was but an unrealised dream,
Reflecting the dawn of a new extreme.
Now, remains of the artist's fading stream.

Painted in layers lie the past,
undying ideas on this wall were cast,
covered up by those who wished to outlast,
but here is the testament that will forever last.

Behind every coat of paint on this wall,
lived an unknown artist.
Behind every brush stroke on this easel,
was a noncomformist.

Bulbul

Whisper, whisper, whisper something,
Deep is the hunger of becoming.
Shadows hold for the fear of ripping,
Shadows cast before the beginning.

Sing, sing, sing aloud,
Melodies that reach the clouds.
Stand tall and stand proud,
Live, before you're wrapped in a shroud.

Whispers of the willow

57

Whispers of the Willow,
Come whisper in my ear,
As sleep evades me and I abandon my pillow,
Come and tell me what I need to hear.

Whispers of the Willow,
Transport me to a haven,
Where the earth sings and where by the winds flow,
Come and comfort me when I'm craven.

Whispers of the Willow,
Guide me in my fragility,
Lend me your wisdom and let your glory show,
Come, whisper and lead me back to tranquility.

Affordable luxury

Come away with me?
Let's be wild and free.
Affordable luxury
And each day a new discovery.

Say what you want,
I know what you mean.
Don't utter a word,
We still get each other.

A far cry from what most are,
But "most" we never were.
No questions asked, no inhibitions,
Is it too much to dream?

The reason my pen bleeds,
I do wish to tell you.
And maybe someday I will,
Until then, my pages fill.